Grit: A Complete Guide on Being Mentally Tough

Author:

Sikandar Sami

Contents

Coarseness: A Complete Guide on Being Mentally Tough

What is Grit?

How about we characterize coarseness. Coarseness is the tirelessness and energy to accomplish long haul objectives. Some of the time you will hear coarseness alluded to as mental strength. Angela Duckworth, a specialist at the University of Pennsylvania, proposes that coarseness is a solid indicator of accomplishment and capacity to arrive at one's objectives.

Duckworth's exploration on coarseness has indicated that...

West Point cadets who scored most elevated on the Grit Test were 60% bound to prevail than their companions.

Ivy League college understudies who had more coarseness likewise had higher GPAs than their friends — despite the fact that they had lower SAT scores and weren't as "keen."

When contrasting two individuals who are a similar age however have various degrees of instruction, coarseness (and not knowledge) all the more precisely predicts which one will be better taught.

Rivals in the National Spelling Bee outflank their companions not as a result of IQ, but since of their coarseness and duty to more reliable practice.

Instructions to Be Mentally Tough

Stage 1: Define what coarseness or mental strength implies for you.

For you, it may be…

going one month without missing an exercise

conveying your work in front of timetable for two days straight

calling one companion to make up for lost time each Saturday this month

Whatever it is, be clear about what you're following.

Stage 2: Build coarseness with little physical successes.

So regularly we ponder how we react to extraordinary circumstances, yet shouldn't something be said about ordinary conditions?

Mental strength resembles a muscle. It should be attempted to develop and create.

Decide to do the tenth rep when it is simpler to simply do nine. Decide to make when it is simpler to expend. Decide to pose the additional inquiry when it is simpler to acknowledge. Demonstrate to yourself — in a thousand small manners — that you have enough guts to get in the ring and do fight with life.

Stage 3: Build solid propensities and quit contingent upon inspiration.

Coarseness isn't tied in with getting a fantastic portion of motivation or fortitude. It's tied in with building the every day propensities that permit you to adhere to a timetable and conquer difficulties and interruptions again and again and over once more.

Intellectually intense individuals don't need to be more brave, more skilled, or more astute — simply more predictable.

Coarseness descends to your propensities. It's tied in with doing the things you realize you should do on a more reliable premise. It's about your devotion to day by day practice and your capacity to adhere to a timetable.

Instances of Grit

Intellectually extreme competitors are more predictable than others. They don't miss exercises. They don't miss tasks. They generally have their partners back.

Intellectually extreme pioneers are more predictable than their friends. They have an unmistakable objective that they progress in the direction of every day. They don't let transient benefits, negative criticism, or riotous timetables keep them from proceeding with the walk towards their vision. They make a propensity for working up the individuals around them — once, yet again and again and over once more.

Intellectually extreme craftsmen, journalists, and workers convey on a more reliable premise than most. They chip away at a timetable, not exactly when they feel inspired. They approach their work like a master, not a novice. They do the most significant thing first and don't evade duties.

The Science of Developing Mental Toughness in Your Health, Work, and Life

Have you at any point thought about what makes somebody a decent competitor? Or then again a decent pioneer? Or on the other hand a decent parent? For what reason do a few people achieve their objectives while others fizzle?

What has the effect?

Generally we answer these inquiries by discussing the ability of top entertainers. He should be the most intelligent researcher in the lab. She's quicker than every other person in the group. He is a splendid business specialist.

However, I think we as a whole know there is something else entirely to the story than that.

Truth be told, when you begin investigating it, your ability and your insight don't play close to as large of a job as you would might suspect. The examination contemplates that I have discovered state that insight just records for 30% of your accomplishment — and that is at the outrageous upper end.

What has a greater effect than ability or knowledge? Mental durability.

Examination is beginning to uncover that your psychological durability — or "coarseness" as they call it — assumes a more significant job than all else for accomplishing your objectives in wellbeing, business, and life. That is uplifting news since you can't do much about the qualities you were brought into the world with, however you can do a great deal to create mental durability.

For what reason is mental sturdiness so significant? Also, how might you grow a greater amount of it?

We should discuss that now.

Mental Toughness and The United States Military

Every year, around 1,300 cadets join the entering class at the United States Military Academy, West Point. During their first summer nearby, cadets are needed to finish a progression of fierce tests. This mid year commencement program is referred to inside as "Monster Barracks."

In the expressions of specialists who have concentrated West Point cadets, "Monster Barracks is purposely designed to test the very furthest reaches of cadets' physical, passionate, and intellectual abilities."

You may envision that the cadets who effectively complete Beast Barracks are greater, more grounded, or more shrewd than their friends. However, Angela Duckworth, a scientist at the University of Pennsylvania, discovered something other than what's expected when she started following the cadets.

Duckworth contemplates accomplishment, and all the more explicitly, how your psychological strength, diligence, and enthusiasm sway your capacity to accomplish objectives. At West Point, she followed an aggregate of 2,441 cadets spread across two entering classes. She recorded their secondary school rank, SAT scores, Leadership Potential Score (which reflects cooperation in extracurricular exercises), Physical Aptitude Exam (a normalized physical exercise assessment), and Grit Scale (which estimates persistence and energy for long haul objectives).

This is what she discovered...

It wasn't quality or smarts or initiative likely that precisely anticipated whether a cadet would complete Beast Barracks. Rather, it was coarseness — the diligence and energy to accomplish long haul objectives — that had the effect.

Actually, cadets who were one standard deviation higher on the Grit Scale were 60% bound to complete Beast Barracks than their friends. It was mental durability that anticipated whether a cadet would be effective, not their ability, insight, or hereditary qualities.

When Is Mental Toughness Useful?

Duckworth's examination has uncovered the significance of mental strength in an assortment of fields.

Notwithstanding the West Point study, she found that...

Ivy League college understudies who had more coarseness additionally had higher GPAs than their companions — despite the fact that they had lower SAT scores and weren't as "savvy."

When contrasting two individuals who are a similar age however have various degrees of training, coarseness (and not insight) all the more precisely predicts which one will be better taught.

Rivals in the National Spelling Bee beat their friends not due to IQ, but since of their coarseness and responsibility to more steady practice.

Furthermore, it's not simply instruction where mental sturdiness and coarseness are helpful. Duckworth and her partners heard comparable stories when they began talking with top entertainers in all fields...

Our theory that coarseness is fundamental to high accomplishment advanced during interviews with experts in venture banking, painting, news coverage, the scholarly world, medication, and law. Asked what quality recognizes star entertainers in their particular fields, these people refered to coarseness or a nearby equivalent as regularly as ability. Indeed, many were awed by the accomplishments of companions who didn't from the outset appear as skilled as others however whose supported responsibility to their aspirations was outstanding. In like manner, many noted with shock that massively talented companions didn't wind up in the more elite classes of their field.

— Angela Duckworth

You have likely observed proof of this in your own encounters. Recall your companion who wasted their ability? What about that individual in your group who pressed the most out of their latent capacity? Have you known somebody who was determined to achieving an objective, regardless of how long it took?

You can peruse the entire exploration concentrate here, yet this is the reality:

In each everyday issue — from your instruction to your work to your wellbeing — it is your measure of coarseness, mental strength, and steadiness that predicts your degree of accomplishment beyond what some other factor we can discover.

As it were, ability is misrepresented.

What Makes Someone Mentally Tough?

It's extraordinary to discuss mental durability, coarseness, and steadiness … yet what do those things really resemble in reality?

In a word, durability and coarseness equivalent consistency.

Intellectually intense competitors are more predictable than others. They don't miss exercises. They don't miss tasks. They generally have their colleagues back.

Intellectually intense pioneers are more predictable than their companions. They have an unmistakable objective that they move in the direction of every day. They don't let momentary benefits, negative criticism, or riotous timetables keep them from proceeding with the walk towards their vision. They make a propensity for working up the individuals around them — once, yet again and again and over once more.

Intellectually intense specialists, scholars, and workers convey on a more steady premise than most. They take a shot at a timetable, not exactly when they feel propelled. They approach their work like a professional, not a beginner. They do the most significant thing first and don't evade duties.

Fortunately coarseness and constancy can turn into your characterizing qualities, paying little mind to the ability you were brought into the world with. You can turn out to be more predictable. You can create superhuman degrees of mental strength.

How?

As far as I can tell, these 3 techniques function admirably in reality...

1. Characterize what mental sturdiness implies for you.

For the West Point armed force cadets being intellectually extreme implied completing a whole summer of Beast Barracks.

For you, it may be...

going one month without missing an exercise

going multi week without eating handled or bundled food

conveying your work in front of timetable for two days straight

pondering each morning this week

crushing out one additional rep on each set at the exercise center today

calling one companion to make up for lost time each Saturday this month

going through one hour accomplishing something inventive each night this week

Whatever it is, be clear about what you're following. Mental strength is a theoretical quality, yet in reality it's attached to solid activities. You can't mystically think your approach to getting intellectually intense, you demonstrate it to yourself by accomplishing something, in actuality.

Which carries me to my subsequent point...

2. Mental strength is worked through little physical successes.

You can't get submitted or steady with a feeble brain. What number of exercises have you missed on the grounds that your psyche, not your body, revealed to you were worn out? What number of reps have you passed up in light of the fact that your psyche stated, "Nine reps is sufficient. Try not to stress over the tenth." Probably thousands for the vast majority, including myself. Also, 99% are because of shortcoming of the psyche, not the body.

— Drew Shamrock

So regularly we believe that psychological durability is about how we react to outrageous circumstances. How could you act in the title game? Would you be able to keep your coexistence while lamenting the passing of a relative? Did you ricochet back after your business failed?

There's no uncertainty that extraordinary circumstances test our fearlessness, diligence, and mental strength ... however shouldn't something be said about regular conditions?

Mental durability resembles a muscle. It should be attempted to develop and create. On the off chance that you haven't propelled yourself in a great many little ways, obviously you'll wither when things get extremely troublesome.

However, it doesn't need to be that way.

Decide to do the tenth rep when it is simpler to simply do nine. Decide to make when it is simpler to expend. Decide to pose the additional inquiry when it is simpler to acknowledge. Demonstrate to yourself — in a thousand little manners — that you have enough guts to get in the ring and do fight with life.

Mental sturdiness is worked through little successes. It's the individual decisions that we make consistently that manufacture our "psychological sturdiness muscle." We all need mental quality, however you can't think your approach to it. It's your physical activities that demonstrate your psychological strength.

3. Mental sturdiness is about your propensities, not your inspiration.

Inspiration is whimsical. Determination goes back and forth.

Mental sturdiness isn't tied in with getting an unbelievable portion of motivation or fortitude. It's tied in with building the day by day propensities that permit you to adhere to a timetable and defeat difficulties and interruptions again and again and over once more.

Intellectually extreme individuals don't need to be more brave, more skilled, or more astute — simply more steady. Intellectually extreme individuals create frameworks that assist them with concentrating on the significant stuff paying little heed to what number of hindrances life places before them. It's their propensities that structure the establishment of their psychological convictions and at last set them apart.

The Proven, Reasonable and Totally Unsexy Secret to Success

There is a typical marvel in the realm of individual money called "way of life creep." It depicts our inclination to purchase greater, better, and more pleasant things as our pay rises.

For instance, say that you get an advancement at work and abruptly you have $10,000 a greater amount of pay every year. As opposed to set aside the additional cash and keep living as would be expected, you're bound to move up to a greater TV or remain at better inns or purchase fashioner garments. Your typical way of life will crawl up gradually and merchandise that were once observed as an extravagance will step by step become a need. What was once far off will turn into your new ordinary.

Changing human conduct is frequently viewed as probably the hardest activity in business and throughout everyday life. However, way of life creep portrays a truly solid way that human conduct changes over the long haul.

Consider the possibility that we adjusted this idea to the remainder of our lives.

Changing Your Normal

How about we show some run of the mill budgetary objectives.

I need to claim fashioner pants.

I need to have a greater house.

I need to drive a quicker vehicle.

Here's the fascinating thing:

These enormous objectives normally occur as a reaction when we have the way to get them going. At the point when our buying power goes up, our buys will in general go up as well. That is way of life creep.

Consider the possibility that comparative reactions could occur in different everyday issues.

Think about these objectives:

I need to include 10 pounds of muscle.

I need to discover an accomplice and get hitched.

I need to acquire six figures for each year.

I need to get a higher score on my test.

I need to possess an effective business.

Imagine a scenario in which we believed that including more muscle or acquiring more cash or showing signs of improvement evaluations would come as a characteristic reaction of improving our typical schedules. As it were, as our typical propensities improved, so would our outcomes.

This thought of marginally altering your propensities until practices and results that were once far off become your new typical is an idea I like to call "propensity creep."

Step by step instructions to Practice Habit Creep

On the off chance that you purchase a larger number of things than your ledger can support, that is not way of life creep. That is called obligation.

Correspondingly, on the off chance that you receive a lot of new practices you can't support, that is not propensity creep. As such, the key is to maintain a strategic distance from the snare of attempting to become excessively quick. Way of life creep occurs so gradually that it is practically vague. Propensity creep ought to be a similar way. You will probably prod your practices along in little manners.

I would say, there are two essential approaches to change long haul practices and improve execution for good.

Increment your presentation by somewhat every day. (The vast majority take this to the outrageous.)

Change your condition to eliminate little interruptions and obstructions. (The vast majority never consider this.)

Here are a few musings on every one:

Expanding your exhibition. You have an ordinary method of living. For instance, your present degree of physical wellness is commonly an impression of how much action you jump on an ordinary day. Suppose that your standard day requires you walk 8,000 stages. On the off chance that you need to improve shape, the standard methodology is begin preparing for a race or exercise more. Be that as it may, the propensity creep approach is add an extremely limited quantity to your standard conduct. State, 8,100 stages for every day instead of 8,000 stages. You can apply this rationale to about any everyday issue. You have an ordinary measure of deals calls you make at work every day, a typical measure of Thank You notes you compose every year, an ordinary measure of books you read every month. In the event that you need to turn out to be more fruitful, more appreciative, or more canny, at that point you can utilize propensity creep to gradually improve those territories essentially by improving the manner in which you live your ordinary day.

Instructions to Get Motivated When You Don't Feel Like It

You've presumably seen that it's difficult to be propelled constantly.

Regardless of what you are really going after, there will undoubtedly be days when you don't want to appear. There will be exercises that you don't want to begin. There will be reports that you don't want to compose. There will be duties that you don't want to deal with. Furthermore, there will be "off days" when your vitality and feelings are in the drain.

These vacillations are a piece of life, and I face these persuasive difficulties the same amount of as anyone else. Be that as it may, for the significant things throughout my life, I've likewise built up a framework for managing these "off days."

We should discuss that framework and how it can assist you with performing great in any event, when you're not feeling roused.

What Baseball Can Teach You About Getting Motivated

I played baseball for a long time, generally as a pitcher. During my last season, I had a quite decent year. I was chosen to the All–Conference group, I was picked as the top male competitor at my college, and I was named to ESPN's Academic All–America group.

However, it wasn't generally that way...

Only a couple of years sooner, I was the main junior to be cut from my secondary school varsity ball club. I played on the JV crew with the entirety of the sophomores and didn't make the varsity group until my senior year ... when I tossed an incredible 11 innings all season.

There are many explanations behind my change from secondary school through school (extraordinary colleagues, training, hard working attitude, etc), yet there is one thing that I figured out how to do in school that I wish I had learned a lot before...

I built up a pre–game schedule that permitted me to perform well, whether or not I was roused or not.

How You Can Use a Pre-Game Routine to Get Motivated

One thing that makes baseball not quite the same as most different games is the sheer number of games that are played. Significant League Baseball crews play 162 games in a season — twice the same number of as the NBA and ten fold the number of games as the NFL. Indeed, even secondary school baseball players will routinely play 40 to 60 games every year.

Such a large number of numerous games, there will consistently be days when you don't feel persuaded, when your body is worn out, or you're simply not intellectually "up" for the game. In that manner, I'd state that baseball is a great deal like life. There will consistently be days when the things that are essential to you feel like a crush.

Yet, the game will be played whether you want to play or not, so you better make sense of an answer for conquering your dreary feelings. I did this by building up a pre-game schedule that would consequently haul me out of a funk and push me over that limit to perform well.

This is what my pre-game routine resembled...

Get a baseball and my glove. Run out to the outfield foul post. Run across along the outfield divider. Stop at the contrary foul shaft. Stretch hips and hamstrings. Run back along the outfield divider. Throw delicately, working back to 75 feet or thereabouts. Head to the warm up area. Stand one stage behind the hill and throw three or multiple times from that point to the catcher. Venture up onto the hill. Throw a couple of pitches without going into the full windup. Begin tossing from the windup for 10 pitches or thereabouts. Toss from the stretch for 10 pitches or somewhere in the vicinity. Get done with one of each pitch (switch up, curve, fastball in, fastball out). Stroll to the burrow.

That entire succession for the most part took 20 to 25 minutes and I did it a similar way each and every time.

While this routine truly warmed me up to play, it likewise — and maybe more critically — put me in the right mental state to contend at an elevated level. Regardless of whether I wasn't groping for the game toward the start, when I completed my pre-game daily practice, I was in "game mode."

As such, it didn't make a difference in the event that I went to the ballpark propelled to play. My pre-game routine began a course of inward occasions that maneuvered me into the correct attitude and made it almost certain that I would succeed.

Suppose you had a normal that could maneuver you into "practice mode" or "work mode", regardless of how little inspiration you had toward the beginning.

In the event that you take a gander at top entertainers in any field, you'll see comparable examples everywhere. NBA players who do something very similar before each free toss shot. Jokesters who recount similar words before they step onto stage. Corporate chiefs who follow a similar contemplation grouping each morning.

Do you think these individuals consistently feel propelled? No chance. There are a few days when the most gifted individuals on the planet wake up feeling like languid fat bombs.

However, they utilize their pre-game schedules to maneuver them into the privilege mental state, paying little heed to how they feel. You can utilize this equivalent cycle to beat your inspiration edge and reliably work out, study, compose, talk, or play out whatever other undertaking that is imperative to you.

Here's the manner by which to do it...

The most effective method to Get Motivated: 3 Steps For Developing Your Routine

Stage 1: A decent pre–game routine beginnings by being anything but difficult to the point that you can't disapprove of it. You shouldn't require inspiration to begin your pre–game everyday practice.

For instance…

My composing routine beginnings by getting a glass of water. So natural, I can't state no.

My weightlifting routine beginnings by putting on my lifting shoes. So natural, I can't state no.

My throwing routine began by getting a baseball and my glove. So natural, I was unable to state no. (Additionally, my mentor would have hollered at me.)

The most significant some portion of any assignment is beginning. In the event that you can't get roused before all else, at that point you'll see that inspiration frequently comes in the wake of beginning. That is the reason your pre–game routine should be inconceivably simple to begin.

For instance, you could make an activity schedule that begins with topping off your water bottle. That way, when you don't want to work out, you can basically let yourself know, "Simply top off the water bottle." Your solitary objective is to begin the everyday practice and afterward proceed from that point.

For additional about the significance of beginning, understood this.

Stage 2: Your routine ought to make you move towards the ultimate objective.

More often than not, your routine ought to incorporate physical development. It's difficult to think yourself into getting spurred.

Here's the reason...

How is your non-verbal communication when you're feeling unmotivated or lacking vitality?

Answer: You're not moving without a doubt. Possibly you're drooped over like a mass, gradually dissolving into the love seat. This absence of physical development is legitimately connected to an absence of mental vitality.

The inverse is additionally obvious. In the event that you're truly moving and drawn in, at that point almost certainly, you'll feel intellectually drew in and stimulated. For instance, it's practically difficult to not feel dynamic, conscious, and invigorated when you're moving.

While your routine ought to be as simple as conceivable to begin, it ought to steadily change into increasingly more physical development. Your psyche and your inspiration will follow your physical development.

Related: physical development doesn't need to mean exercise. For instance, on the off chance that you will likely compose, at that point your routine ought to carry you closer to the physical demonstration of composing.

Stage 3: You have to follow a similar example each and every time.

The main role of your pre-game routine is to make a progression of occasions that you generally perform before doing a particular errand. Your pre–game routine tells your brain, "This is the thing that occurs before I do ___."

In the end, this routine turns out to be so attached to your exhibition that by just doing the everyday practice, you are maneuvered into a psychological express that is prepared to perform. You needn't bother with inspiration, you simply need to begin your daily practice.

In the event that you recall the article on the 3 R's of Habit Change, at that point you may understand that your pre-game routine is essentially making an "update" for yourself. Your pre-game routine is the trigger that launches your propensity, regardless of whether you're not persuaded to do it.

This is significant on the grounds that when you don't feel persuaded, it's frequently an excess of work to make sense of what you ought to do straightaway. At the point when confronted with another choice, you will frequently choose to simply stop. Notwithstanding, the pre-game routine takes care of that issue since you know precisely what to do straightaway. There's no discussing or dynamic. You simply follow the example.

Instructions to Get Motivated: Make Excellence a Routine

You can prepare yourself for progress similarly just as you can prepare for disappointment.

Today you might be stating, "I should be spurred to complete anything," however I ensure that it doesn't need to be that way. On the off chance that you've instructed yourself to accept certain restrictions, at that point you can likewise instruct yourself to get through them.

The examples that you rehash consistently will inevitably frame the personality that you have confidence in and the moves that you make. You can change your personality and become the sort of individual who needn't bother with inspiration to perform well.

This is the reason it's so basic to do your pre-game schedule inevitably, not exactly when you're battling with an absence of inspiration. These little practices strengthen your great propensities and the emotions that accompany them. Quite soon, your pre-game routine won't just be a trigger that launches your propensity, yet in addition a token of what you're moving in the direction of and the kind of individual you are turning out to be.

This is the distinction between moving toward life as an expert or a novice.

The most effective method to Fall in Love With Boredom and Unlock Your Mental Toughness

Dominance is never a mishap. You can win the lottery and become rich short-term, yet nobody has ever aced their art by some coincidence. Regardless of whether we are discussing competitors, specialists, or scholastics, the story is the equivalent. On the off chance that you need to satisfy your latent capacity, at that point you should rehearse a particular ability for quite a while with noteworthy consistency.

Paul Erdos, the phenomenal mathematician, distributed more than 1,500 papers before setting up himself as an idea chief.

Celebrated authors put in 10 years of undervalued work before winning acknowledgment.

Milo of Croton, the unbelievable Greek grappler, gotten a youthful calf consistently until he created extraordinary quality.

Some way or another, top entertainers in any art make sense of an approach to become hopelessly enamored with weariness, placed in their reps, and accomplish the work.

Obviously, at whatever point "specialists" share anecdotes about effective individuals they frequently forget about a key element of the story. How, precisely, do top entertainers become hopelessly enamored with weariness? Maybe more significant, how might you begin to look all starry eyed at weariness when you're attempting to fabricate a propensity that you realize you ought to do, yet you would truly prefer not to do.

Let me share two methodologies that work for me.

Step by step instructions to Fall in Love With Boredom

Initially, there is next to no expectation for experiencing passionate feelings for a propensity that you really scorn. I don't know any individual who genuinely detests a movement and some way or another experiences passionate feelings for doing it. It doesn't make any sense. It's hard to abhor something and be enamored with it simultaneously. (Your ex doesn't tally.)

Suppose you loathe turning out to be, however you know it's beneficial for you. On the off chance that you need to begin to look all starry eyed at the fatigue of heading off to the exercise center, at that point you have two alternatives.

Choice 1: Increase your capability at the assignment.

Indeed, even errands that you are acceptable freely feel dull a few days, so envision the daunting struggle you're battling on the off chance that you are continually attempting to accomplish something that you don't feel gifted at. The arrangement? Get familiar with the essential things of your assignment and praise the little successes and upgrades you make. With our exercise model, suppose you buy Starting Strength and figure out how to do a legitimate deadlift or seat press. Rehearsing these new abilities in the exercise center can be fun and making minuscule upgrades every week gathers speed. It's a lot simpler to go gaga for accomplishing something again and again in the event that you can anticipate gaining ground.

Alternative 2: Fall in adoration with a consequence of the assignment instead of the undertaking itself.

How about we be genuine: there are a few things that we ought to do that are continually going to be a problem. Running runs may be a model. Not many individuals anticipate setting their lungs ablaze.

I find that I have more accomplishment in circumstances like these when I move my concentrate away from the real undertaking and toward an outcome. Now and then this is an immediate aftereffect of the propensity I'm attempting to perform. Different occasions, it's an outcome that I concoct. For instance, you can make a game out of not missing exercises regardless of whether you abhor the exercise itself. Suppose you have done two run exercises in succession. You will probably begin to look all starry eyed at turning into the sort of individual who doesn't miss exercises. You're not stressed over how you perform. You're not stressed over in case you're getting quicker. You're not stressed over getting well defined abs or some other sort of result. Generally, you're not in any event, considering the exercise. Rather, you're basically centered around keeping your exercise streak alive.

This is fundamentally the Seinfeld Strategy applied to work out. Your lone objective is to "not break the chain." By moving your concentrate away from the movement you hate, you're allowing yourself a chance to go gaga for the fatigue of adhering to the streak (something you do appreciate).

What I Do When it Feels Like My Work Isn't Good Enough

Initially, it was simple. There was no weight. There were no external eyes. There were no desires.

At the point when I began composing, I wrote in a private report for longer than a year prior to I distributed my first article on JamesClear.com. I expounded on what I needed to expound on. I composed in light of the fact that I needed to get my considerations down. I composed in light of the fact that I had a feeling that I expected to compose.

Following a couple of long stretches of sharing my work freely, things started to change.

As I built up a group of people, I saw that I started making a decision about my work. Before all else, I was only glad to get my thoughts down on paper, yet now I felt like they must be "acceptable" thoughts. I started contrasting new articles with my most mainstream ones. I was continually estimating all that I composed against my inner norm of good and awful—despite the fact that I didn't know precisely what that implied.

Fortunately, I didn't let my self-question prevent me from composing. I figured this was a piece of the inventive cycle for any individual who made things reliably. I revealed to myself that judgment and self-question was only a cost that I needed to pay to proceed with the travel and make better work.

As it were, this is valid. Everybody manages self-question—craftsmen, makers, business visionaries, competitors, guardians. In any case, as it were, I wasn't right. Self-question isn't a cost you need to pay to turn out to be better. We should discuss why.

The Inner Game of Tennis

I simply wrapped up a book that has been on my perusing list for a long while, The Inner Game of Tennis (book recording) by Timothy Gallwey. It is a book about existence, not simply tennis.

Specifically, there was one statement from Gallwey that made me delay and reexamine my initial a long time of composing and self-question.

"At the point when we plant a rose seed in the earth, we notice that it is little, however we don't scrutinize it as "rootless and stemless." We treat it as a seed, giving it the water and sustenance expected of a seed. At the point when it first shoots up out of the earth, we don't censure it as juvenile and immature; nor do we scrutinize the buds for not being open when they show up. We remain in wonder at the cycle occurring and give the plant the consideration it needs at each phase of its turn of events. The rose is a rose from the time it is a seed to the time it passes on. Inside it, consistently, it contains its entire potential. It is by all accounts continually during the time spent change; yet at each state, at every second, it is completely okay all things considered."

— Timothy Gallwey

Aspiration and happiness are not alternate extremes, yet we regularly wrongly think that they are contradictory. From one viewpoint, specialists disclose to us that we ought to be careful, centered around the present, and substance with our carries on with paying little mind to the outcomes. Then again, mentors and champions disclose to us that effective individuals outwork every other person, that we should never be fulfilled, and that carelessness is unfortunate.

The rose seed, in any case, is both substance and goal-oriented.

As Gallwey says, at no time are we disappointed with the present status of the rose seed. It is completely OK at every second. However, it is likewise extraordinarily yearning. The rose seed grows constantly. It is continually trying to get to the following level. Consistently it is pushing ahead, but, consistently it is similarly as it ought to be.